THE COLLEGE DICTIONARY

A BOOK YOU'LL ACTUALLY READ!

ILLUSTRATED BY:
Cathy Law

ABSENT: The notation generally following your name in a class record.

3

ADMISSIONS OFFICE: Where they take you to get you to admit you've mooned the keynote speaker during "new student weekend."

ANATOMY: One of those classes that sounds vaguely risque' until you find out what it really involves.

4

BIOLOGY: A class that is located suspiciously near the cafeteria.

BOOK: A depository of knowledge which a student will try to stay awake long enough to read the night before finals.

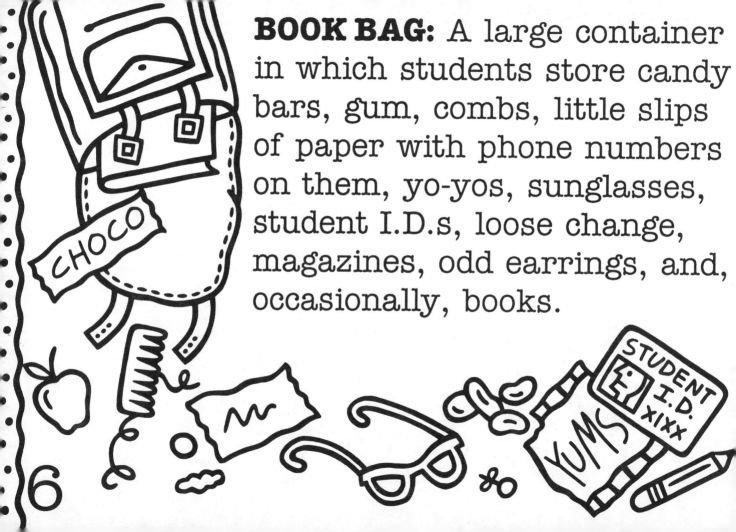

BOOK BAG: A large container in which students store candy bars, gum, combs, little slips of paper with phone numbers on them, yo-yos, sunglasses, student I.D.s, loose change, magazines, odd earrings, and, occasionally, books.

6

CAFETERIA: From two Latin words, "Cafe," meaning "Place to eat," and "Teria," meaning "to wretch."

CAFFEINE: One of the four basic food groups.

CALL: What you can't do because your stupid roommate has to go over every stupid detail of every stupid day with their stupid hometown sweetheart.

BLAH BLAH BLAH and YAK YAK YAKITTY BLAH BLAH and YAK YAK and BLAH BLAH...

8

COACH: A kind of teacher who rewards successful "students" with a new Corvette.

CUM LAUDE: How students in southern universities call dogs named "Laude."

9

D-MINUS: A pretty good grade.

DORM: Student residence located only a few convenient miles from 8 a.m. classes.

10

DORMROOM: A small, closet-like area, inhabited by a pair of incompatible people.

EDUCATION BUDGET: Money you allocate each month for movies and magazines.

EGGHEAD: 1) A brainy student who studies all the time and gets straight A's. 2) That same student, once you've dropped eggs on him from the roof of the science lab.

12

EXTRA CREDIT: What you wish you had on your credit card.

F: A grade that can usually be altered to look like a "B" on a test paper.

FAN-CICLES: Dim-bulb guys who arrive back at the dorm hooting and shivering after attending a football game with no shirt on in the hopes of appearing on TV.

14

FINALS: A series of tests that precede a big party.

GEEK: One who actually finds humor in a professor's joke.

16

GESUNDHEIT: Your answer to every question on your German final.

GRADE: Unrealistic and limited measure of academic accomplishment.

GUIDANCE COUNSELOR: The person who will spend four years guiding your college career, only to be "just as surprised as you" when you're short 17 credit hours in your major with one-half a semester left.

GUITAR: The musical instrument your former roommate played prior to the mysterious accident in which it was shattered.

19

HALLWAY: A convenient waterslide included on every floor of the dorm.

20

HEARTY HANDSHAKE: The climax of many social outings, often described back at the dorm as a breathless naked romp through society's taboos.

HIGH-RISE: 1) A tall building. 2) The least coveted type of undergarment to get on a panty raid.

HUNGER: Condition produced by five continuous minutes of studying.

22

I: One of the two most often used words in the vocabulary of a cheerleader. The other is "Me."

IMMATURE: An adjective used to describe anyone who seems to be having more fun than you.

23

IVY: Green, leafy plant growing up the side of the dorm that thrives on spilled beverages and tiny taco chip fragments.

24

JACUZZI: Large warm tub of bubbling water that those thoughtful hotel managers near campus don't lock up very securely at night so they're practically open to the public.

JANITOR: The guy with the low-slung jeans who mumbles while he cleans old gum and soaking wet napkins out of the dorm water fountain on Monday morning.

JELLY BEAN: As close to eating a vegetable as many students ever get.

JOB:

(Sorry...didn't mean to scare you.)

27

JOY: The kind of soap you're reduced to using in the shower until you get a check from your parents.

JUNIOR VARSITY: The team everybody supports, but nobody goes to watch.

28

KAPPA: What members of sororities or fraternities wear on their headas.

KITCHENETTE: A small, thin person working in the cafeteria kitchen.

KAPPA

HEADA

29

KLUTZ: What you discover your lab partner is when you ask him to slowly pour the sulphuric acid into the beaker you're holding.

30

LAB: A room full of icky, funny-looking creatures, and the dead frogs they dissect.

LETTERMEN: Scholarship athletes who proudly wear letter sweaters proclaiming the vowel or consonant they have mastered.

31

LIBERAL ARTS: See: "Would you like fries with that?"

LOUNGE: Any area in a dorm, union or classroom building where the only furniture that isn't soiled, ripped or scarred is immediately stolen.

33

MAJOR: Area of study that no longer interests you.

MIDNIGHT OIL: What you make popcorn in.

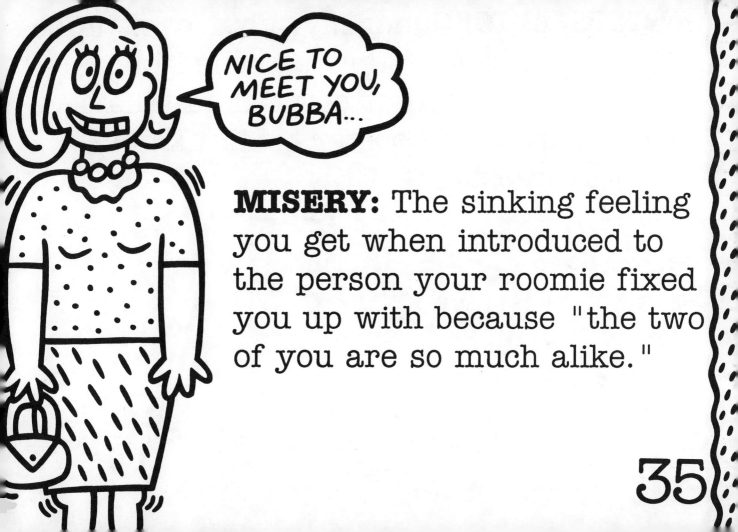

NICE TO MEET YOU, BUBBA...

MISERY: The sinking feeling you get when introduced to the person your roomie fixed you up with because "the two of you are so much alike."

35

NICKNAME: Generally, your own name with the suffix "ster" attached in a forced, awkward attempt at familiarity. For example, "Bobster," "Hankster," or "Georgester."

"NO": The response that guys who spend most of their time in the gym lifting weights might put on a true-false test.

37

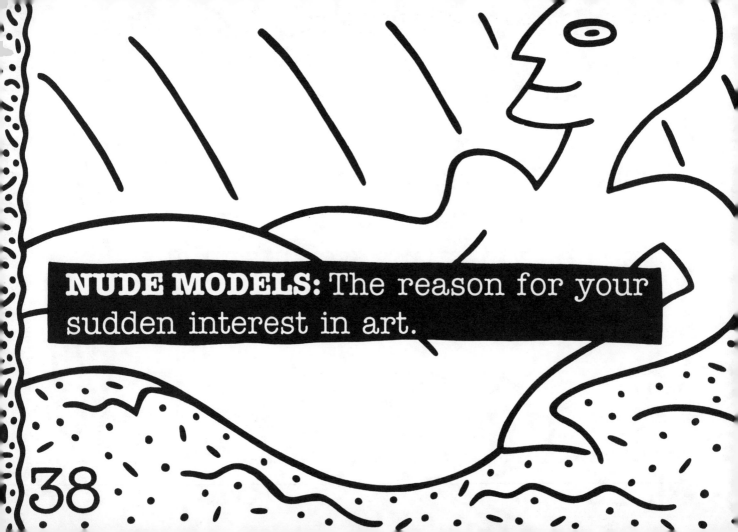

NUDE MODELS: The reason for your sudden interest in art.

38

OFF-CAMPUS PARKING: Ample extra parking, usually found in an adjoining county.

OTHELLO: Unless you're an English major, who really cares?

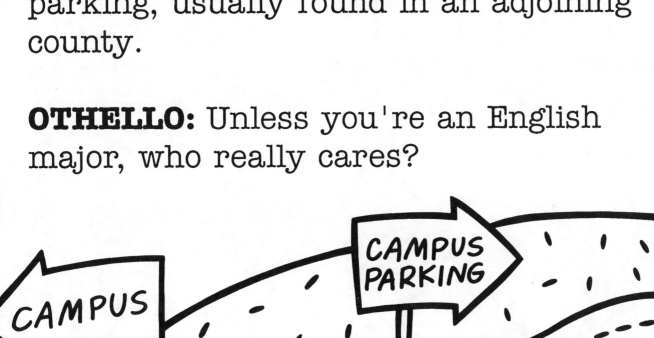

OUT: Where your roommate always is when one of the 35 clubs she belongs to calls with a very important message.

PAPER: Your rendering of the Cliff Notes.

41

POSTER: An inexpensive way to decorate a dorm room while making people think you've been to foreign lands and done things you never have.

PRE-LAW: The major of a person who will end up in sales.

42

QUADRANT: 1)Any of four quarters into which something is divided. 2) To express anger while in the quad.

43

QUANTUM PHYSICS: Course you now regret signing up for just because the line was short at registration.

QUARTER: The most coveted form of currency on campus.

REGISTER: 1) To enroll in class. 2) What you will operate in New York or Los Angeles the rest of your life if you're a drama major.

REUNION WEEKEND: A brief time when returning alumni demonstrate how quickly you lose it once you're out of school.

HEY BABE!

CLASS OF '72

45

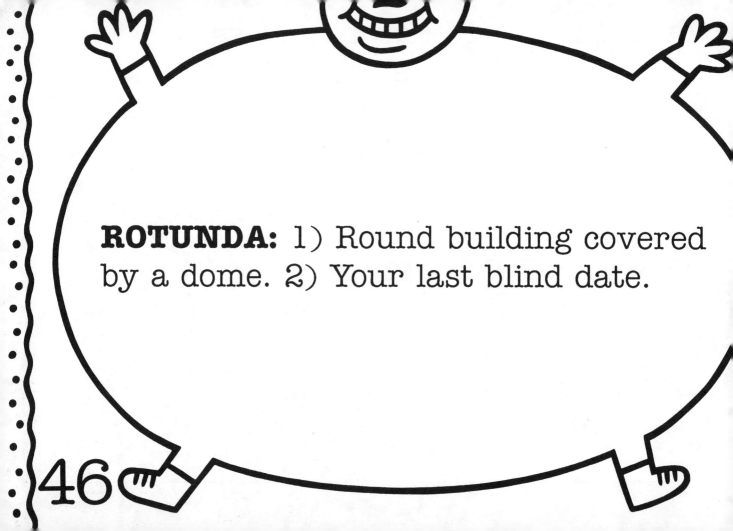

ROTUNDA: 1) Round building covered by a dome. 2) Your last blind date.

46

RUNNING BACK: 1) An important member of the college football team. 2) What you're doing if you're clear across campus from your dorm at five minutes before curfew.

47

SOAP: 1) What you add to laundry, if you have it. 2) A TV show you schedule class attendance around.

STUDENT ATHLETE: See: "Contradiction in terms."

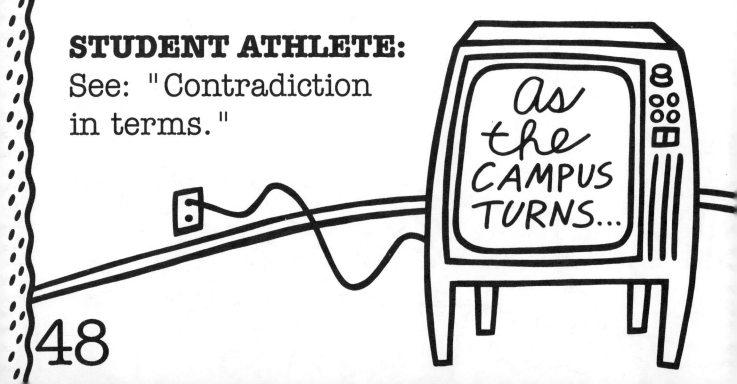

48

STUDY: That activity you are always busy at your desk doing on the morning of Parents' Visitation Weekend.

49

STUDY GROUP: A collection of "D" students looking for an "A" student to sponge off of the night before an exam.

SUMMER SCHOOL: A viable alternative to a summer job.

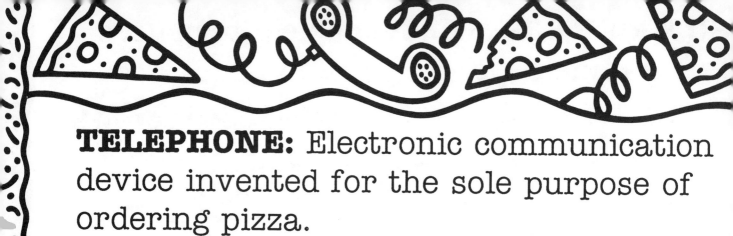

TELEPHONE: Electronic communication device invented for the sole purpose of ordering pizza.

TUBA: The band instrument played by the dedicated insomniac in the dorm room next to yours.

52

TUTOR: Superior student who serves two important functions: First, to assist you in difficult studies. Second, to make you feel really stupid by condescendingly asking "You don't even know **that**?!"

UNDECIDED: The most popular major on campus.

UNDERWEAR: What you keep buying to avoid doing laundry.

VACUUM: A cleaning appliance that you and your roommate might as well sell and split the money.

VALEDICTORIAN: The student you wish you had sat next to and befriended.

VICE SQUAD: A group of uniformed officers who seem to be under the impression that they were invited to your dorm party.

VENDING MACHINE: A coin-operated device for dispensing breakfast, lunch and dinner.

VICTOR: Your football team's weekly opponent.

VICTORY: A rarity: A three-syllable word that cheerleaders can spell.

WEEKEND: Two-day period during which your growling stomach makes you really wish you'd signed up for the seven-day meal plan.

WHIZ KID: Your college nickname. But not for the reason people think.

WINDELLAS: Name of the circus family you can run away and join when your parents find out how much you put on their charge card.

HOME sweet HOME

WINTER: When the air-conditioning in your dorm finally kicks in.

WORK-STUDY: Two things not done by a majority of students.

WRISTWATCH: That device on your arm that lets you know which class you're currently late for.

61

X-RAY: A medical technique that will display cafeteria meatballs up to 10 years after they are eaten.

XYLEM: We're not going to tell you this. You should know this. You took biology, didn't you? Were you asleep that day, or what?

MEATBALL X-RAYS

1 YEAR 3 YEARS 7 YEARS 10 YEARS

YALE: 1) A well-known ivy-league university. 2) What Southern cheerleaders do.

63

YEARBOOK: A book containing student pictures that will keep getting nerdier as the years go by.

1969

1975

1987

YESTERDAY: When the 12-page paper you started tonight was due.

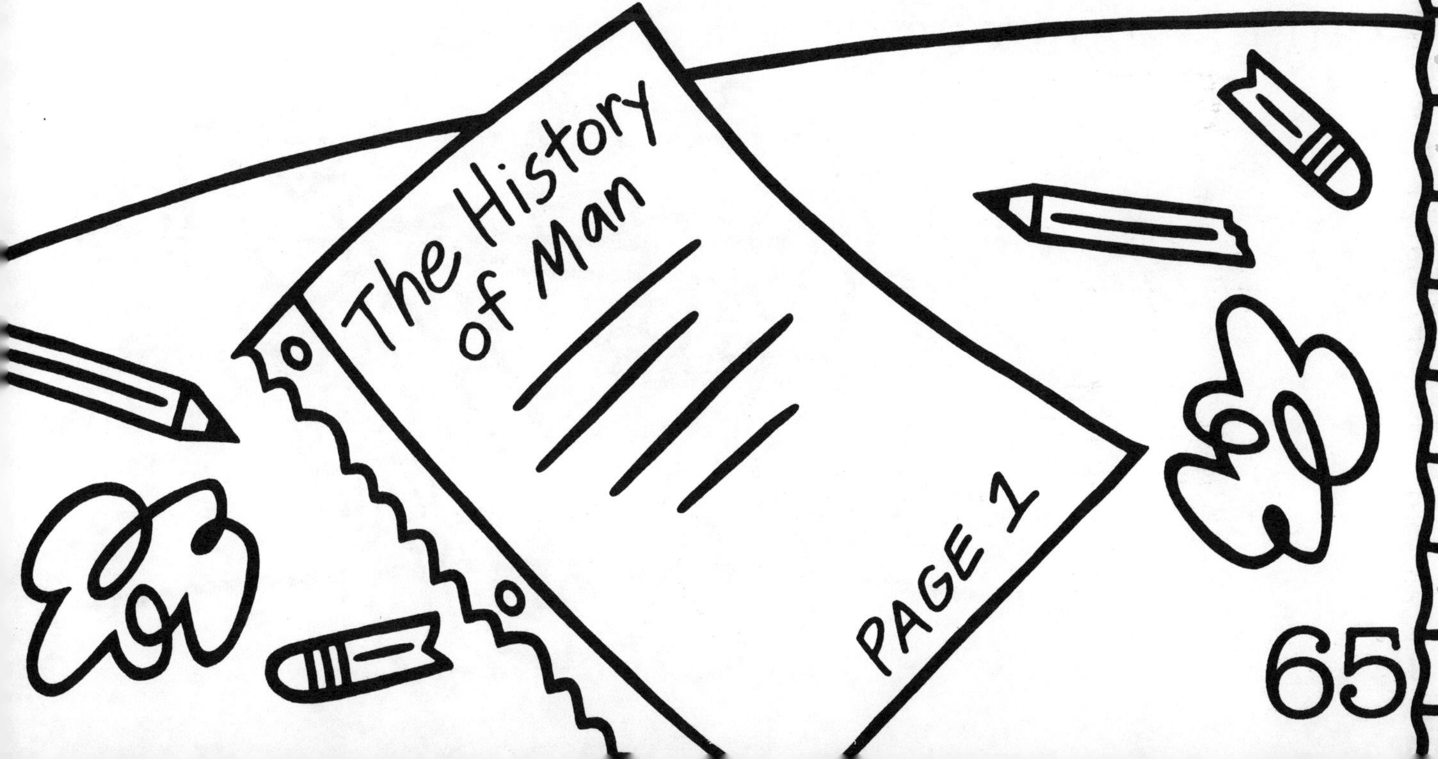

The History of Man

PAGE 1

YIELD SIGN: Dormitory wall decoration you "purchased" around three in the morning, with the help of two buddies and a hammer.

ZEPPELIN: 1) A large blimp. 2) Still the best band for playing air guitar in one's underwear.

ZERO: The number of times you've gotten to eat most of the pizza you ordered.

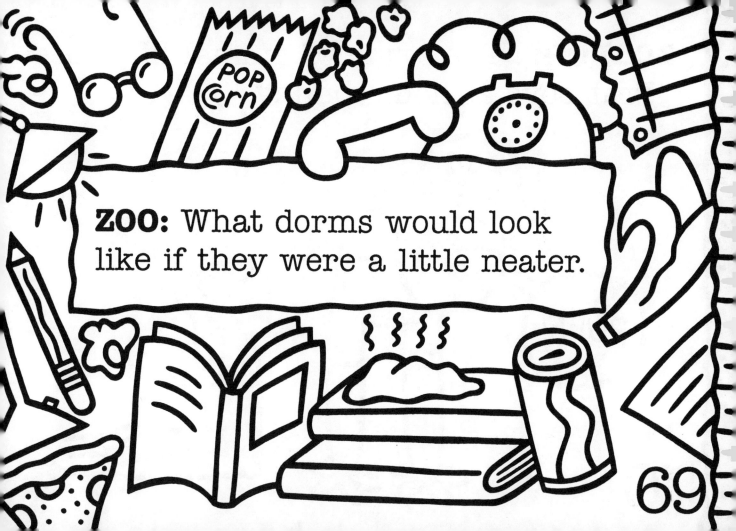

ZOO: What dorms would look like if they were a little neater.

69

ZOOLOGY: The study of animal life. (See: "Frat boys at homecoming.")

Other books from
SHOEBOX GREETINGS
(A tiny little division of Hallmark)

HEY GUY, ARE YOU: A) Getting older? B) Getting better? C) Getting balder?

GIRLS JUST WANNA HAVE FACE LIFTS: The Ugly Truth About Getting Older.

DON'T WORRY, BE CRABBY: Maxine's Guide to Life.

WAKE UP AND SMELL THE FORMULA: The A to No Zzzzz's of Having a Baby.

STILL MARRIED AFTER ALL THESE YEARS.

THE GOOD, THE PLAID AND THE BOGEY: A Glossary of Golfing Terms.

EVERYTHING YOU ALWAYS WANTED TO KNOW ABOUT STRESS... but were too nervous, tense, irritable and moody to ask.

FRISKY BUSINESS: All About Being Owned by a Cat.

40: THE YEAR OF NAPPING DANGEROUSLY.

RAIDERS OF THE LOST BARK: A Collection of Canine Cartoons.

THE MOM DICTIONARY.

THE DAD DICTIONARY.

THE WORLD ACCORDING TO DENISE.

WHAT...ME, 30?

THE OFFICIAL COLLEGE QUIZ BOOK.

YOU EXPECT ME TO SWALLOW THAT? The Official Hospital Quiz Book.

WORKIN' NOON TO FIVE: The Official Workplace Quiz Book.

THE FISHING DICTIONARY: Everything You'll Say About the One That Got Away.